IMAGES
of America

MONTGOMERY
COUNTY

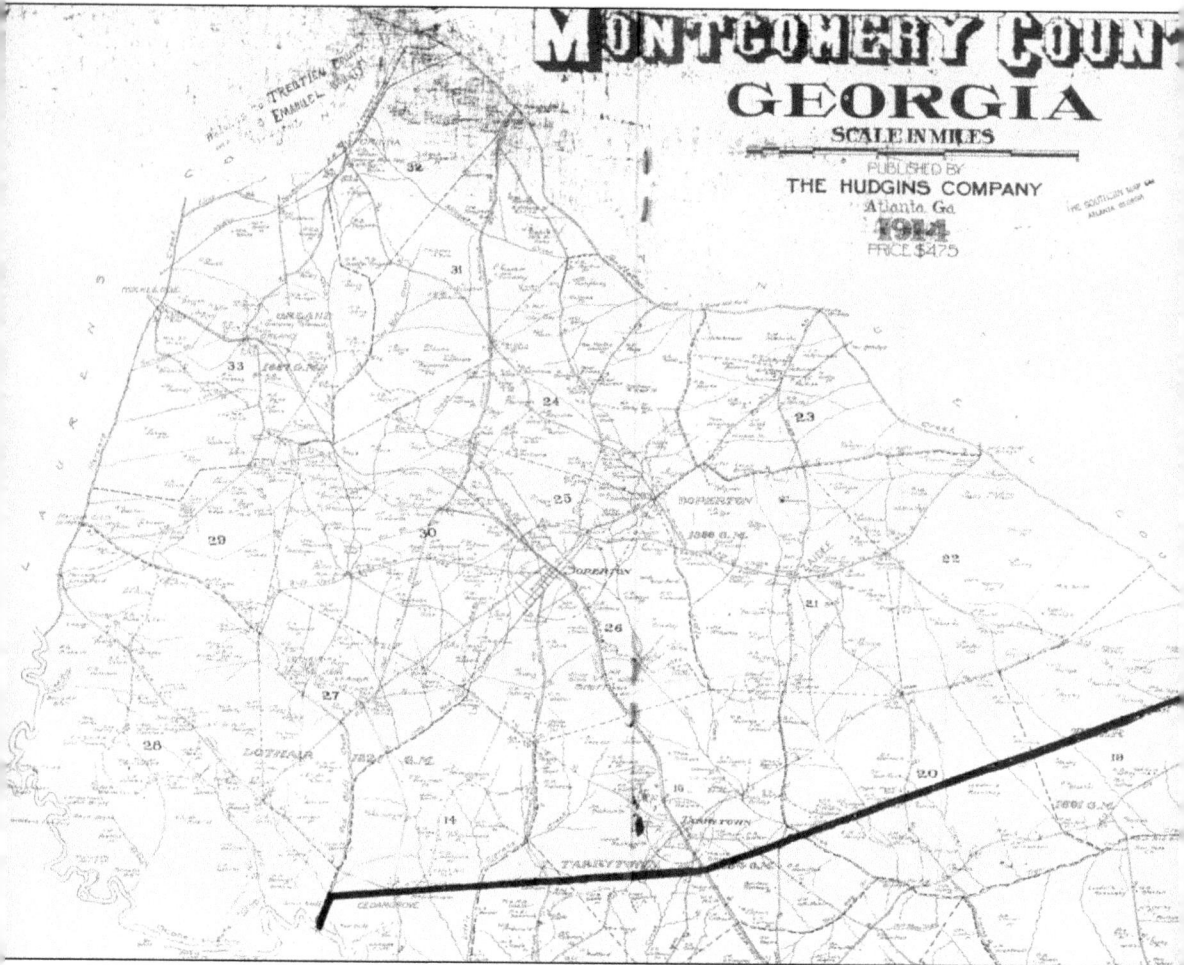

This 1914 map of Montgomery County depicts each house and its occupant's name, making it an important tool for learning where people were living at that time. (Courtesy of the Georgia State Archives.)

ON THE COVER: Timber rafting down the Oconee and Altamaha Rivers was a common occurrence in the late 1880s and early 1900s. The huge yellow pine trees of the area's virgin forests were sawed down and stripped, then hauled to the riverbanks on large, high-wheeled oxcarts. They were then strapped together to form temporary rafts on which men rode to shipping yards in Darien and Savannah, where the logs were loaded on ships for European destinations. The men then bought certain needed supplies or gifts for their families and walked all the way back home, camping along the way. (Courtesy of the Montgomery County Office of Clerk of Courts.)

IMAGES
of America

MONTGOMERY COUNTY

Larry R. Braddy and
Olivia Williamson Braddy

ARCADIA
PUBLISHING

Published by Arcadia Publishing
Charleston, South Carolina

Library of Congress Control Number: 2010922357

For all general information, please contact Arcadia Publishing:
Telephone 843-853-2070
Fax 843-853-0044
E-mail sales@arcadiapublishing.com
For customer service and orders:
Toll-Free 1-888-313-2665

Visit us on the Internet at www.arcadiapublishing.com

This volume is dedicated to Moses Algerine "M. A." and Reba Burns Braddy, both born in Montgomery County and descendants of the oldest families of the county—the Williamson, Adams, Hamilton, and Collins families. Born in 1917 to Henry Algerine Braddy and Estella Collins, M. A. passed away in January 2008. Reba Carmen Burns Braddy was the daughter of Virgil Henry Burns and Mary Delilah Williamson. M. A. and Reba, devout Christians, reared seven children on ancestral land that they farmed. Reba Braddy was well-known to attend and pray for the sick and led many to Christianity. (Authors' collection.)

CONTENTS

ACKNOWLEDGMENTS

A compiled work of this nature cannot be possible without the interest and efforts of others, both past and present, who, possessed with a deep love of local history and its preservation, have passed on their valuable knowledge to us.

We especially wish to thank the staff of Keith Hamilton, Montgomery County Clerk of Courts, for allowing us to reproduce images from the Dwight Newsome collection, which is maintained in that office; Newsome spent years documenting local history and was instrumental in the creation of the original Montgomery County Historical Society. There are several other historians and genealogists in the area, known and unknown, who have contributed greatly to our knowledge of the pioneering of this old county; among them are Jack Ladson, Edna Earle Morris, Benjamin Jackson, Ray Tapley, and J. Clayton Stephens Jr. Moses Coleman Jr. should certainly be recognized and commended for the years he and his assistants spent searching for and documenting cemeteries of the area; their books are a valuable resource for locating the final resting places of our people. We are grateful to all those who have treasured and preserved these precious photographs of their families, most of them now gone on, as well as snapshots of local scenes and places, many of which are no longer in existence, and who so generously allowed us to include them in this book. We have noted these contributors with a credit line following the captions; all other images are from the authors' personal collections.

We also wish to give special credit to our paternal grandmothers, Estella Collins Braddy and Onie Calhoun Williamson, both talented storytellers, who instilled in us a pride of family and times long past. They planted in us the seed for our continued hunger for knowledge of our people and their history. And lastly, we want to thank one another for our mutual and longtime enthusiasm for learning about and maintaining the histories of our respective families; working together on this project has been a culmination of our combined years of study.

It is important for our children to learn from the past, and by viewing these images, it is hoped they will more clearly understand the hardships their forebears endured and feel challenged to continue the documentation and preservation of the rich history of this noble county.

INTRODUCTION

Created by a legislative act on December 19, 1793, from the southern portion of Washington County, Montgomery County is bound by the Oconee River on the east and the mighty Altamaha River to the south, formed at the "Forks" where the Ocmulgee and the Oconee Rivers meet head-on, creating a "T" shape. Named for Richard Montgomery, an American general killed in an attack on the British in Quebec during the American Revolution, Montgomery County has had its boundaries redrawn 18 times. Only the northern part of modern-day Montgomery County was part of the original county. Long considered a wasteland of pine barrens and bogs, early settlers deemed Montgomery County only suitable for grazing livestock, rather than the production of crops. The original county of Montgomery essentially remained a wilderness inhabited by the Yamassee, a tribe of the Creek Confederacy, until the close of the American Revolution in 1787. While the British crown and the Spanish in Florida vied for control of the area, especially the Yamassee village of Tama at the mouth of the Altamaha and the land along the Oconee and Ocmulgee Rivers, the Yamassee switched sides frequently, mounting a fierce resistance to European encroachment upon their ancestral hunting grounds, culminating in their eventual annihilation. Subsequent to the establishment of the colony of Georgia under James Edward Oglethorpe in 1733, several trading posts were established at the Forks, including the "Bosomworths' Old Trading Place," established in 1746 by the half–Native American Mary Musgrove and her husband, Thomas Bosomworth, with support of the British crown and approval of the Creek Nation; however, these settlements were abandoned after the British government discontinued support. The Forks served as a pivotal location; several strategic trails and roads crossed the Altamaha at this junction (*History of Montgomery County Georgia to 1918*, by Robert Scott Davis Jr., 192). Native Americans frequently crossed the Oconee River into Montgomery County until the early 1790s, usually at Bell's Ferry, several miles north of the Forks; occasionally, Creek and Seminole Indians raided settlements in the county up until the early 1800s.

The early settlers of old Montgomery County were rugged frontiersmen who wrestled a meager livelihood from the soil of the wiregrass hills and valleys, having come from Virginia, North and South Carolina, and the piedmont region of Georgia, usually by wagon train. These "Scotsmen of the Pines" cut the virgin timber. Among the early Scotch-Irish to settle Montgomery County were settlers with the surnames McGregor, McArthur, McAllister, McAlpin, McLemore, McLendon, McLeod, McNatt, McQueen, McMillan, McCall, McCrimmon, McDaniel, McDonald, McIntosh, McIntyre, McGill, McBride, McRae, Calhoun, Hamilton, Sullivan, Mosley, Wilkes, Adams, Collins, Williamson, Phillips, Gillis, Moore, and others. These early settlers to Montgomery County cleared the pine barrens to plant crops of corn, tobacco, and cotton. Then they hauled the pine logs to the Oconee and Altamaha Rivers and strapped them together to create large rafts, which they floated to the ports of Darien and Savannah for shipment abroad to markets in Europe and Asia. The pine trees also served the settlers in the construction of the primitive log cabins in which they dwelt, as well as barns in which they stored their crops and housed their

7

livestock. Later, pine trees played a significant role in the naval stores or turpentine industry of the county. The economy of Montgomery County over the centuries has been intertwined with the production of pine trees. Rustic log cabins and barns, antebellum houses, Victorian homes with wraparound porches, and other edifices attest to the significance of the yellow pines of old Montgomery.

Families who now reside in Montgomery County are eighth- and ninth-generation descendants of the pioneers who settled the county during the 1790s and early 1800s. The slave population of Montgomery County on the eve of the War Between the States was almost half of the total population. Thus, African Americans have contributed significantly to the county's history. African Americans were instrumental in building the communities of Mosley Town and the Isle of Hope. Like its forbears, the populace of Montgomery County today is deeply religious, composed of hardworking folks who take real pride in their ancestry. Timber production remains significant in the local economy, just as it did during the era of the rafters. Likewise, the production of cattle remains a viable source of income for the farmers of the county, just as it did when the cattle of the early settlers roamed the hills and woods of the pine barrens. Many of the fields in which the early pioneers grew cotton, corn, and tobacco have now returned to pine forests like those that covered the area down through the centuries. The county's farmers now produce onions and soybeans on a larger scale, while the family farm has almost disappeared. Many of the old fields have been planted with pecan orchards, which have become a major money crop, especially since the influx of the Mexican population. The vintage photographs found in these pages portray the lives of farmers, merchants, and their families engaged in everyday life, school, and worship down through the decades. Like their ancestors, the families of the county work hard, rear their children to respect traditional values, place a great premium on the education of their children, and engage in community activities.

One

OUR PEOPLE: OUR HERITAGE

This image of Asa Lemuel Adams (1809–1891) was taken from a tintype made in his latter years, when he was blind. Asa was a son of Penelope Adams (c. 1770–c. 1850). His father was probably Lemuel Williamson, who married Penelope in 1811. Both Penelope and Lemuel were living on land grants in Montgomery County by the 1790s; she migrated from North Carolina, and he came over from South Carolina. In 1828, Asa married Louisa Phillips, daughter of William Con Phillips and Nancy Phillips. The little cabin where Asa and Louisa reared their 11 children still stands in a wooded area of the county. (Courtesy of Jean Griffin Moore.)

Samuel Daniel Smith (1886–1965) was a son of Council Benjamin Smith and Sarah Ellen "Sallie" Moore. This picture was made the day he married Lottie Rico (1889–1933), of Carolton, Mississippi. They were the parents of 10 children. This family owned farm property in the Kibbee community. (Courtesy of Martha Smith Gibbs.)

Dressed up in their Sunday best are, from left to right, Henry Palmer, Azle Lampp (1892–1914), Charlie Collins (1887–1980), ? Palmer, Ezrabell Lampp, and ? Palmer. Azle and Charlie were married in 1912. (Courtesy of Myrtice Collins O'Connor Hamilton.)

William John McBride and Floy Minnick are pictured in this late 1880s photograph, probably taken on their wedding day.

In this c. 1890 photograph is Andrew Johnston "John" Williamson (1870–1921), son of John A. Williamson and Dicy Phillips. He married Lula Elizabeth Moore (1874–1943), and they were the parents of 12 children. In 1920, this family lived on a farm near Longpond. (Courtesy of Royce Phillips.)

This photograph of little Earline Calhoun was probably taken at the party her parents gave her on her fourth birthday, November 12, 1906, just eight days before her death, caused by complications from a tonsillectomy. She was a daughter of Charlton Henry Calhoun and Sarah "Sally" Brooks. Her grieving parents laid her little body to rest in the old Calhoun Cemetery near Tarrytown. (Courtesy of Joseph Hilton Memory Jr.)

A son of David Keen Collins and Mariah Jennett "Jane" Cobb and a native of Tattnall County, Sikes Collins (1852–1915) came to Montgomery County as a farm laborer and, in 1883, married Mary Ann Elizabeth Adams (1851–1901), daughter of William Riley Adams and Mary "Polly" Hamilton. They had five children: Minnie, Elmira Estella, Charles Hilton, Lillian, and Saphronia. After his wife's death, Sikes then married Bianca Ladson Warnock (1879–1970), daughter of Isaac Larrimore Ladson and Pinky Grace Elizabeth Connell. They were the parents of six more children: Colon Fletcher, Isaac Lee, Effie Ruth, Lorita Irma, Lewis, and Sikes Jr.

Three generations of Braddy men are posed here together. Seated is Moses Algerine "M. A." Braddy (1917–2008). Standing on the left is grandson Ryan Bennett Braddy, and on the right is son Larry R. Braddy. M. A. Braddy was the son of Henry Algerine Braddy and Stella Collins of the Kibbee community. He married Reba Carmen Burns, daughter of Henry Virgil Burns and Mary Delilah "Lila" Williamson.

Benjamin Chess "B. C." Moxley (1875–1962) and his wife, Emma Black (1877–1941), lived in eastern Montgomery County on the Taylor Springs Road. Here the couple reared 10 children. B. C. and Emma are buried in Hamilton Hill Cemetery. (Courtesy of Rubie Nell Moxley Sanders.)

Benjamin Franklin "Bennie" Palmer (1872–1960) is pictured here beside his second wife, Almedia Hall (1896–1970). Bennie was one of 12 children born to Jarred Edward Palmer and Martha Ann Hamilton. His first wife was Lavenia Williamson (1873–1918). He and both wives are buried in the Jack Williamson Cemetery near Kibbee. (Courtesy of Mary Achenbach Wilkes.)

14

Benjamin S. "Ben" Warnock (1887–1978) was the son of Christopher Columbus "Lum" Warnock and Margann Adams. In 1907, he married Eunice Conaway (1891–1986), and their 10 children were named Ira Felton, Estus A., Julius Franklin, Nellie, Benjamin "Bennie," Ethel, Dovie Lee, Emmit Emerson, William Eschol "Bill", and Joye. (Courtesy of Faye Conaway Waller.)

Bianca Ladson Collins (1879–1970), second wife of Sikes Collins, is shown here (second row, fourth from left) surrounded by 10 of the Sikes Collins children. Bianca was a daughter of Isaac Larrimore Ladson and Pinkey Grace Elizabeth Connell. She had first married William Joseph Warnock, and that marriage ended in divorce; after Sikes Collins's death, she married J. J. Isdale, which also ended in divorce. Bianca died in Thomas County, Georgia.

In this rare 1940s photograph are all six sons of Henry Algerine Braddy and Elmira Estella Collins. Standing in front of their parents' home are, from left to right, William Steelie, Vandorn "Van," Cecil B., Julian "Juke," Moses Algerine "M. A.," and Wallace Athel.

16

William Henry "Bill" Moxley was born in 1846, probably in Washington County, Georgia, to William A. Moxley and Emily Hall. About 1870, he married Mary Elizabeth "Lizzie" West (1849–1920). After living a few years in Emanuel County, they made their home in Montgomery County in the Taylor Springs community, where they reared a large family. (Courtesy of Rubie Nell Moxley Sanders.)

A traveling photographer arranged this c. 1895 portrait of the Bill and Lizzie Moxley family, taken in front of their home. (Courtesy of Rubie Nell Moxley Sanders.)

Robert Lee Burns (1868–1940) was born in Washington County to Jordan Minter Burns and Olive Page. He is shown here with his wife, Martha Jane Ellis (1868–1947), daughter of John Ellis and Mary Elizabeth "Babe" Brantley. Robert and Martha began married life in Johnson County, moving to Montgomery County after 1900, where they raised 14 children. This family lived in Higgston for many years.

Born in Montgomery County to James Irving Calhoun II and Nancy Clarissa Connell, Burrell Rogers Calhoun (1858–1925) had the same name as his paternal grandfather. (His father had been named for an uncle.) A graduate of Mercer University and the University of Georgia, he taught school in Laurens County for several years before moving to Eastman, Dodge County, in 1882 to practice law. In 1888, he married Mary Frances "Mollie" Clark (1866–1908), daughter of Matthew Clark and Mary Hendley. Their resting place is Woodlawn Cemetery in Eastman. (Courtesy of Bobby T. Moore.)

Jesse Edge (1891-1966) was a son of Jason Edge and Penelope Bedgood. He married into the old Cauley family and he and his wife, Lizzie (1900-1929), daughter of Cadwell Cauley and Annie Smith, reared several children on their farm. After her death, he married Lizzie White. Pictured are Jesse Edge and his first wife, Lizzie Cauley, with their eldest child, Otis. (Courtesy of Annie Lou McGahee Edge.)

Shown in their early years together are Cecil Thomas Blocker (1906–1977) and his wife, Mary Zelma Palmer (1909–2008). The couple operated a small filling station and grocery store near Kibbee. Both are descended from several of the oldest families in Montgomery County, including the Adams, Hamilton, Phillips, and Williamson families. After Cecil's death, Zelma married again, first to Lamar McDaniel and then to R. G. Hardy. Zelma was considered one of the foremost genealogists of the Hamilton family in Georgia and old Montgomery County. She published her work in a book in the 1970s entitled *Hamiltons and Related Lines*. (Courtesy of Bobby T. Moore.)

Posing in this studio picture is Charles Malcolm "Charlie" Adams (1865–1900), son of William Riley Adams and Mary "Polly" Hamilton. In 1890, he married Mollie Hutcheson (1876–1958), and they were the parents of Henry, Harris Leon, James Elza, Ethel H., and Riley Lutrell. (Courtesy of Bobby T. Moore.)

A son of Josiah Hamilton and Mary "Polly" Poole, Charles Stringer Hamilton was born in Montgomery County in 1831 near present-day Kibbee. His first child was Miles Willis Calhoun, whose mother was Hannah Elizabeth Calhoun, daughter of Burrell Rogers Calhoun and Mary Darley. In 1878, "for natural love and affection," Charles Hamilton deeded 150 acres of land to the children of Miles Calhoun. In 1857, Charles married Susan Darley, and she died childless in 1862. He married Ruth Ann Elizabeth Williams in 1865, and they were the parents of 11 children. Charles served in the Georgia General Assembly. His home still stands in the Kibbee community. (Courtesy of Bobby T. Moore.)

Charles J. "Charlie" Phillips (1875–1933) was the son of Norman Phillips and Laura Ann Mosley. He married Amanda McBride (1872–1914), daughter of John Rainey McBride and Adeline McGar, in 1902. Following her death, he married Minnie Burns (1897–1919), daughter of Robert Lee Burns and Martha Jane Ellis. Charlie and Minnie lived in eastern Montgomery County and farmed ancestral land there. They are pictured shortly before her death in 1919. After Minnie's death, Charlie married Ruby Calhoun, born in 1904 to Leander "Nat" Calhoun and Mary Hortense Sapp. Allegedly, Charlie lost his money in his old age and spent most of his time digging huge wells on his farm in search of the lost treasure. Bands of gypsies frequently encamped on his farm. It is not known if they were responsible for the missing money.

Clarence Aubrey Adams (1883–1967) was a son of William Wiley "Captain" Adams and Melissa Delma Peterson. He is pictured here with his first wife, Dicey Herrington (1890–1933), a daughter of Anthony Manning Herrington and Frances Augusta Curl. (Courtesy of Robert C. "Bob" Adams.)

This group, pictured in 1983, represents five generations of the Burns-Galbreath family. Seated at left is Mary Delilah "Lila" Williamson Burns. Standing behind Lila is her daughter, Marjorie Christine "Margie" Burns Galbreath. Seated at right is Margie's daughter, Melrose Galbreath NeeSmith. Standing behind Melrose is her son, Ken Sheppard, and the baby Melrose is holding is Ken's daughter, Heather Sheppard. (Courtesy of Margie Burns Galbreath.)

Playing together in front of their father's car are, from left to right, siblings DeAvis, DeAnne, and Miles "Buddy" Blaxton, the children of Lester Miles Blaxton and his wife, Dorothy DeAlva Palmer. (Courtesy of DeAnne Blaxton Shiplett.)

Pictured are Daniel Webster Galbreath (1847–1931) and his descendants at a birthday celebration held for him on July 4, 1929, at the old home place in the Sharpe Spur community near Alston in the southern end of the county. Among the group are his sons, Thomas, George, Henry, and Elijah, and their children; spouses of Daniel's children are not in the picture. (Courtesy of Margie Burns Galbreath.)

Shown is one of only two cars in Uvalda in 1916. J. B. and Georgia Wallace Brogdon and their children, Wallace (foreground) and Milton, went by Vidalia to have Leverett's Studio staff come and take this picture. (Courtesy of the Montgomery County Office of Clerk of Courts.)

Duncan Alexander McRae (1869–1962) was a son of Phillip McRae and Jane McKinnon. He was one of several Montgomery County men responsible for the organization of the Mount Vernon Bank in 1900. He began as a director of the bank and later held other offices, including president. A successful businessman, he accumulated large land holdings. In 1903, he was married to Victoria Wooten (1880–1976), and they made their home on Railroad Avenue in Mount Vernon, where they reared their four children, Elizabeth, Jane, Harold Wooten, and Duncan Alexander Jr. (Courtesy of Philip McRae.)

In this c. 1930 pose are siblings Lucian C. Warnock (in front) and, from left to right, Edward C. "Eddie" Warnock, Elma Warnock Spivey, and James W. Warnock. They were children of Christopher Columbus "Lum" Warnock and Anna Ladson. (Courtesy of Kimball Warnock.)

The children of Eliza Collins Adams (1804–1905), widow of Matthias Adams (1800–1855), gave their mother a family dinner in honor of her 100th birthday on January 1, 1904. Seven of her children were able to attend this elaborate affair. Pictured left to right are (first row) John W. Adams, Sarah Elizabeth "Sally" Adams Hamilton, Eliza "Little Grandma" Collins Adams, Julia Ann Adams Clark, and William Thomas Ezekiel "W. T. E." Adams; (second row) Matthias Jasper Adams, Robert R. Adams, and Charles Daniel Adams. This well-attended event was held at the Matthias Adams home place.

Eliza Collins Adams, the wife of Matthias Adams, was the daughter of Joseph Collins Jr. and Susannah Summerlin of Tattnall County. She was referred to affectionately as "Little Grandma" and lived to be nearly 102. According to an article in the *Montgomery Monitor*, at the time of her death, she was the oldest inhabitant of Montgomery County.

J. B. and Liza O'Connor are posing for this picture, probably on their wedding day in 1896. James Benjamin O'Connor Jr. (1875–1961) was a son of James Benjamin "Jim" O'Connor, an Irish immigrant of unknown parentage, and his wife, Clarissa Ann Hamilton, daughter of Josiah Hamilton and Mary "Polly" Poole. Eliza Grace Palmer (1874–1968) was a daughter of Joseph Palmer and Amanda Mantha Adams. J. B. O'Connor was a well-known and successful businessman of many ventures in Montgomery and Toombs Counties. (Courtesy of Mark Burns.)

Shown at right is the Peter Gailette Ware family. Posing from left to right are (first row) Guy, Effie, and John Ware; (second row) Susan "Sally," Luther Earl, and Peter G. Ware. Peter Gailette Ware was born in 1864, the youngest of 12 children born to Nicholas and Matilda Ware of Wilkes County, Georgia. Their eldest son, Luther Earl Ware (1886–1966), married Obie Varnadow (1884–1967). This family moved to Montgomery County in the 1920s, living near Kibbee, where they farmed for many years. (Courtesy of Martha Smith Gibbs.)

A large reunion of descendants of Matthias and Eliza Collins Adams was held in 1904 at the old log house on the Matthias Adams homeplace. The affair was featured

prominently in the *Montgomery Monitor.*

Addie Calhoun was born in Montgomery County in 1891 to Miles Willis Calhoun and Susan Anna Darley. In 1907, she married Norman Trull, son of Joseph Benton Trull and Mary "Polly" Powell, and they were the parents of 10 children. (Courtesy of Bobby Tyson.)

Good friends dressed up and had this studio picture taken in the 1920s. On the left is Frances Beaty, daughter of Daniel B. "Dan" Beaty and Lecy Ann Phillips. On the right is William McKinley "Bill" Mitchum, son of Neill Mitchum and Lucinda Bell "Lucy" Nunn. In 1940, Frances married Eschol Frederick Fountain, son of Charles "Charlie" Fountain and Theodosia "Dosia" Palmer. (Courtesy of Linda Wilkes.)

Joseph Hilton Memory (1907–1990) is shown at the age of 16 with his bird dog. A son of John Anson Memory and Minnie Williamson, he married Helen Calhoun (1912–2009), daughter of Charlton Henry Calhoun and Sarah "Sally" Brooks. (Courtesy of Joseph Hilton Memory Jr.)

Grover Cleveland "Cleve" Wilkes (1894–1980) is pictured here relaxing on his front porch to read the newspaper. A son of William Thomas Wilkes and Queen Ann Nunn, Cleve married Vennie Sarah Phillips (1905–1989), a daughter of Thomas Jefferson Phillips and Quincey Lee Blaxton. Cleve Wilkes was known for his excellent methods of farming and maintenance of timberland. (Courtesy of Linda Wilkes.)

Susan Anna Darley (1858–1945) was born in Montgomery County, said to be a daughter of James Henry Darley and Catherine Barlow. In 1875, she married Miles Willis Calhoun (1855–1919) and they made their home near Tarrytown, where they reared 12 children.

George Edward West (1871–1945) is portrayed here around the beginning of the 20th century. Having come to Montgomery County from North Carolina with a sawmill operation, he married Minnie Collins (1883–1972), daughter of Mary Ann Elizabeth Adams and Sikes Collins, and became the patriarch of a large family whose descendants still reside in Montgomery County today. (Courtesy of Myrtice Collins O'Connor Hamilton.)

Posing together here are brothers James Grady Blaxton (left) and William Mack Blaxton (center), sons of George Silas Blaxton and Sara Ella Nunn, with their cousin, William McKinley "Bill" Mitchum, son of Lucinda Bell Nunn and Neill Mitchum. (Courtesy of DeAnne Blaxton Shiplett and Mary Achenbach Wilkes.)

Ida Wilkes and a friend are enjoying a Sunday buggy ride in the Alston community. This picture was made in the early 1900s. (Courtesy of Wayne Wilkes.)

This 1920 photograph shows the entire family of George Silas and Sara Ella Nunn Blaxton, except a son, Alexander Grover Blaxton, who apparently was taking the picture. From left to right are (first row) Rufelt Tosh Blaxton, Roy Phillips, Lester Miles Blaxton, George Silas Blaxton, John Lee Blaxton, Sara Ella Nunn Blaxton, Quincey Lee Blaxton Phillips, Tommie Phillips, Estelle Blaxton, and Ethel Beckum; (second row) George Dewey Blaxton, William Mack Blaxton, Alexander Grover Blaxton Jr., James Grady Blaxton, Louise Blaxton, Ellie Field Blaxton, Ellie Field Blaxton Jr., Alice Columbia Humphrey Blaxton, Sara Laura Blaxton, Vennie Phillips Wilkes, Lucy Belle Blaxton, Mamie Beckum Blaxton, and Cyril Roger Blaxton. (Courtesy of DeAnne Blaxton Shiplett.)

This youthful photograph of Benjamin Stewart "Bennie" Calhoun (1861–1951) was probably made in the 1880s, prior to his marriage to Mary Susan Frances Kent (1872–1900), daughter of William James Washington Kent and Martha Ann Beckworth. Bennie, a son of Samuel Hargroves Calhoun and Mary Lucinda Hamilton, was one of the first trustees in 1904 of Union Baptist Institute, which later became Brewton-Parker Junior College, and was organizer and president of the Farmers Bank in Glenwood in 1906. In his early years, he also was a dealer in lightning rods throughout the state. Bennie and Mary are buried with her family in Glenwood City Cemetery.

Shown standing in the foreground between the graves of her parents in Pinecrest Cemetery, Vidalia, with an unidentified woman is Sema Morris Wilkes (1905–2002). Born Sema America Morris to William Lawton Morris and Sarah Emily Taylor, of the Aimwell community, she married Lois Herman Wilkes (1905–1990), son of Arvy L. Wilkes and Janie Bell McDonald. Sema Wilkes was well known throughout the state as the owner and operator of the popular Mrs. Wilkes' Boarding House Restaurant in Savannah, where for many years she prepared and served traditional Southern dishes and always began each meal in her restaurant with a simple prayer.

Harris Leon Adams (1892–1973), son of Charles Malcolm "Charlie" Adams and Mollie Hutcheson, was the operator of the Coca-Cola bottling plant in Vidalia for many years. Here he is seen around 1913 hauling drinks in a wagon before cars or trucks were used for delivery. (Courtesy of Marion Witt Hutcheson.)

Shown around 1908 with his wife and firstborn child, Martha, is John Hampton Jr., born in 1877 to John Hampton and Elizabeth Thornton. His maternal grandparents were Elisha Thornton and Hannah Elizabeth Calhoun. John Hampton Jr. married Murtie Key, daughter of John Nelson Key and Willie Ann McCall, and reared a large family. (Courtesy of Joseph R. Hampton.)

Standing together in this 1950s
picture are the daughters of Andrew
Jackson Williamson II (1844–1910)
and his wife, Lecy Ann Phillips
(1848–1917). Not necessarily listed
in order, they are Teresa (Hall),
Ruth Elizabeth "Ruthie" (Adams),
Effonia "Effie" (Hamilton), Minnie
(Memory), Almeda (Davis), and Mary
Jane (Blocker-Adams). Another sister,
Lavenia (Palmer), had died in 1918.
(Courtesy of Mary Achenbach Wilkes.)

Harold Wooten McRae, born in 1912
to Duncan Alexander McRae and
Victoria Wooten, is pictured here
as a young man. He later married
Virginia Peacock. The McRae family
was prominent in Mount Vernon
and associated with banking and
commerce. (Courtesy of Philip McRae.)

Mary Ann Delilah Adams Williamson and daughter Lucille pose here around 1918. Mary was the daughter of William Thomas Ezekiel Adams and Mary Delilah Browning. She married Millard Milton Williamson of Montgomery County. Lucille was their youngest child, a beautiful redhead. (Courtesy of the Williamson family)

John Neal Connell (1859-1937) was a son of Bazzel Connell and Christian Ferguson of the Bear Creek community. He married Martha Blount (1868-1937), daughter of William Benjamin Blount and his first wife, and they were the parents of 13 children. (Courtesy of George King II.)

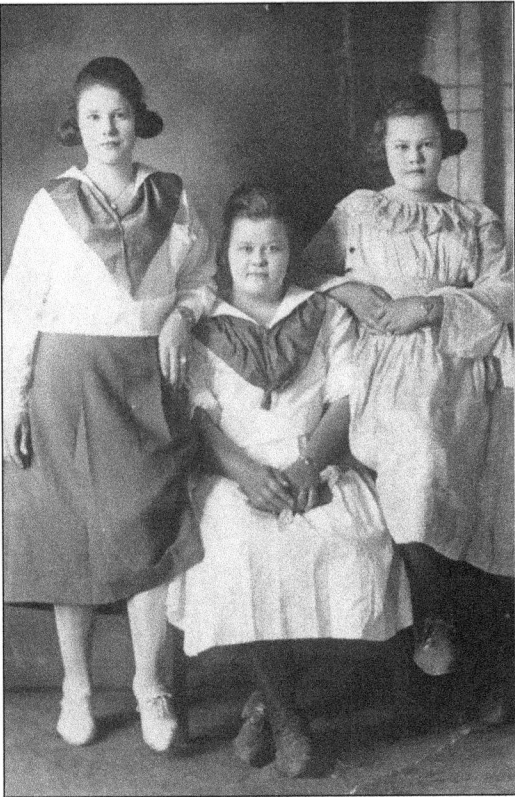

Standing here are sisters Lucy Belle Blaxton West (left) and Sarah Laura "Dottie" Blaxton Webber, daughters of George Silas Blaxton and Sara Ella Nunn. Seated is their niece, Vennie Sarah Phillips Wilkes, daughter of Thomas Jefferson Phillips and Quincey Lee Blaxton. (Courtesy of Mary Achenbach Wilkes.)

Florence Herndon (1858–1942) and Moses Algerine Braddy (1847–1918) are portrayed here during the 1870s. Florence was the daughter of Henry Herndon and Samantha Miller of Montgomery County; Moses Algerine was the son of Oliver Bennett Braddy and Elizabeth Smith. This couple, who lived at the intersection of Braddy Road and the Old Louisville Road, were the parents of 14 children whose descendants continue to live in Montgomery County today.

Shown with John Robert Adams (1875–1978) and helping him to celebrate his 100th birthday are his nephews, from left to right, Cecil Earnest Williamson (1911–1984) and Alphy Lanier Williamson (1898–1988). The younger men were the sons of Millard Milton Williamson and Mary Ann Delilah Adams. John Robert Adams's home was in Charlottesville.

Pictured during a special visit to get acquainted with his great-great-great-uncle, John Robert Adams, is Ryan Bennett Braddy. Although Ryan looks a little uncertain, he soon warmed up to his elderly host. This picture was made in 1974. Ryan is the great-great-grandson of John Robert Adams's sister, Mary Ann Delilah Adams Williamson.

Bazzel Connell (1824–1916) is pictured here in his elderly years. He was a son of John Connell, Revolutionary soldier from Pennsylvania, and his wife, Clarissa Hamilton. Clarissa's father, Stewart Hamilton, also fought in the Revolution. He married Clarissa Stringer in Wake County, North Carolina, before migrating to Montgomery County, Georgia around 1802. Bazzel Connell fought for the Confederacy in the War Between the States. He first married Christian Ferguson (1828–1897), daughter of John Ferguson and Mary Currie. He married his second wife, Ava, in 1898.

41

Eleven of the 14 children of Moses Algerine and Florence Herndon Braddy are shown here at a family reunion in the 1950s at the old Calhoun Millpond near Tarrytown, now called Warnock Pond. Many of their descendants continue to live in Montgomery County.

William Wiley "Captain" Adams (1853–1943) and Melissa Delma Peterson (1846–1897) are shown in this photograph taken shortly after their marriage. Captain Adams was the son of William Riley Adams and Mary "Polly" Hamilton of Kibbee. Melissa was the daughter of Daniel Peterson and Mary O'Neal. (Courtesy of Bobby Tyson and Bobby T. Moore.)

William Thomas Ezekiel "W. T. E." Adams and his first wife, Delilah Browning, are portrayed here during the 1870s. W. T. E. was the son of Matthias and Eliza Collins Adams of the Charlotte community. Delilah was a daughter of George R. Browning and Emaline Mariah Chaney, who lived near Glenwood.

Vandorn "Van" and Lucille Palmer Braddy are shown here in front of the Henry A. Braddy homeplace in the early 1940s. Van (1914–1998) was a son of Henry Algerine Braddy and Stella Collins; Lucille (1914–1994) was a daughter of Charles R. "Charlie" Palmer and Maggie Garner. (Courtesy of the Braddy family.)

Posing here are James Isaac Fountain (1819–1906) and his wife, Sabrina Chambers (1832–1895). They were the progenitors of the Fountain family in Montgomery County. (Courtesy of Robert Calhoun.)

Standing in front of their home are some members of the Jimmy Adams family. James Riley "Jimmy" Adams (1856–1944) was a son of William Riley Adams and Mary "Polly" Hamilton. In 1877, he married Lucinda Mamie Calhoun (1859–1919), daughter of Samuel Hargroves Calhoun and Lucinda Hamilton. (Courtesy of Royal Sullivan.)

Lavenia Williamson (1873–1918) is pictured here in her teens. She was a daughter of Andrew Jackson "Jack" Williamson and his wife, Lecy Ann Phillips. In 1889, she married Benjamin Franklin "Bennie" Palmer (1872–1960), son of Jarred Edward Palmer and Martha Ann Hamilton. After Lavenia's death, Bennie married Almedia Hall. (Courtesy of Mary Achenbach Wilkes.)

Onie Calhoun Williamson (1895–1984) had her picture made at Sapp's Studio in Vidalia wearing her dress made for the nation's bicentennial in 1976. That year, she wore the dress to a costume party hosted by the Rural Letter Carriers' Convention, held annually at Jekyll Island. Onie had carried the mail on the Oak Park route throughout the time her husband was away in the U.S. Merchant Marines during World War II. He resumed his postal duties upon his return, but she always enjoyed attending the conventions. Onie was a daughter of Benjamin Stewart Calhoun and Mary Susan Frances Kent. She was first married in 1912 to Frederick William Kea, a lawyer in Dublin; she divorced him and, in 1917, married her cousin, Gaston Beauregard Williamson (1894–1962).

Willie Lee Moore (1901–1994) is pictured with his wife, Mary Esta Phillips (1907–1989), and their first son, Willie Hartridge Moore. Willie Lee Moore was a son of William Edward and Frances Isabel Moore, and Mary Esta was a daughter of Daniel Hartridge Phillips and Nora Lee Stewart. (Courtesy of Doris Davis Moore.)

Sisters Loumedia (1884–1920), at left, and Lucinda Palmer (1878–1958) pose for their picture around 1900. Daughters of Jarred Edward Palmer and Martha Ann Hamilton, Loumedia "Medy" married William Richard Hilton in 1910, and Lucinda Lee "Cenia" married Sidney Livingston "Sincey" Morris in 1903. (Courtesy of Mary Achenbach Wilkes.)

Christopher Columbus "Lum" Warnock (1857–1939) is pictured here with his first wife, Margann Adams (1863–1899), and their children. Lum Warnock was a son of Simeon Warnock and Lucy Lamb, and Margann was a daughter of William Riley Adams and Mary "Polly" Hamilton. They lived in the Kibbee community, where they reared a large family. After Margann's death, Lum married Anna (Goff) Ladson. (Courtesy of Faye Conaway Waller.)

Malcolm Mosley was a patriarch of the Mosley family who lived in the Mosley Town community. He was a farmer and brick mason and one of the founders of the Mosley Town Church of God in Christ. He married Patsy Phillips. (Courtesy of Helen Mosley Collins.)

Patsy Phillips and her husband, Malcolm Mosley, reared nine children in the Mosley Town community. They were both very active in their church and community. (Courtesy of Helen Mosley Collins.)

Martha Ann Hamilton Palmer (1842–1921) was the youngest daughter of Josiah Hamilton and Mary "Polly" Poole of Kibbee. She was the twin of Andrew Jackson Hamilton (1842–1895), who married Arcadia "Kate" Mosley. Martha Ann married Jarred Edward Palmer (1844–1928), and they were the parents of 12 children. (Courtesy of the Hamilton family.)

Dudley Green "Cap" Warnock (1888–1979) is pictured here with his wife, Alma Braddy (1892–1968), and three of their children. Cap was a son of Green John Warnock and Margaret Glover; Alma was a daughter of Moses Algerine Braddy and Florence Herndon. This family was active in farming and timber stores. (Courtesy of Faye Conaway Waller.)

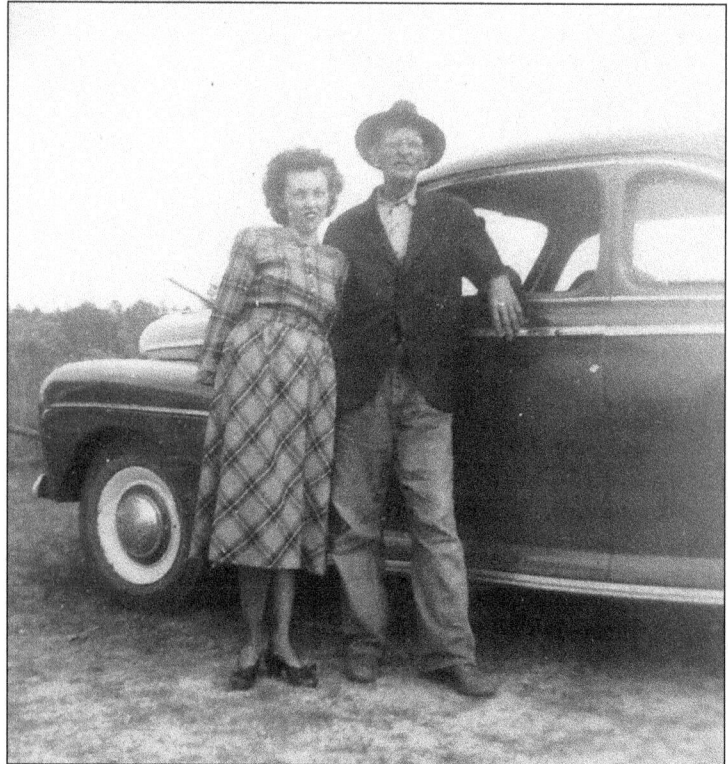

Shown in this 1950 picture are Anderson William "Bill" Stanford (1880–1951) and his daughter Lois Stanford (1922–2008) at their residence, located in the part of Treutlen County that was previously in Montgomery County. Bill was the son of John David Stanford (1846–1918) and Georgia Walker (1853–1905). Bill Stanford married Emma Gillis (1885–1961), a daughter of John Gillis. (Courtesy of Bobby Stanford.)

Pictured here is William Riley Adams II (1873–1894), son of William Wiley "Captain" Adams and Melissa Delma Peterson. He was killed in an explosion at the gristmill owned by his grandfather, William Riley Adams, for whom he was named. (Courtesy of Bobby Tyson.)

Mary Ann Elizabeth "Lizzie" Adams (1851–1901) is portrayed here as a young woman. The daughter of William Riley Adams and Mary "Polly" Hamilton of Kibbee, she married Sikes Collins (1852–1915) in 1883. They lived in a log home on Thompson Pond Road, where many of their descendants still live today.

Martha "Mattie" Warnock (1888–1920) was a daughter of Christopher Columbus "Lum" Warnock and Margann Adams. In 1915, she married Oscar Ocran Rewis (1882–1920), son of James Buel Rewis and Josephine Hamilton; she was his third wife. Their children were Nadine and Robert Lee Rewis. (Courtesy of Faye Conaway Waller.)

Shown here in midlife are Millard Milton Williamson (1862–1939), son of Andrew Jackson Williamson and Lecy Ann Moore, and his wife, Mary Ann Delilah Adams (1869–1939), daughter of William Thomas Ezekial Adams and Delilah Frances Browning. They lived on a large farm in a portion of Montgomery County that became Toombs in 1905.

Minnie Williamson Memory (1878–1956) is pictured here at her birthday celebration in 1952. Minnie was a daughter of Andrew Jackson "Jack" Williamson and Lecy Ann Phillips; she married John Anson Memory (1865–1927) in 1896. (Courtesy of Kay Memory Claxton.)

Pictured (standing) are Mae Ruth Palmer and her mother, Mollie Hutcheson Palmer. Mae Ruth married Paul Wendell Calhoun in 1935. Seated on the porch are Hazel (left) and Ethlyn Witt, children of Henry Castellaw Witt and Ethel Adams. (Courtesy of Marion Witt Wilkes Hutcheson.)

The Moses Algerine Braddy family is pictured here at their homeplace around 1914. From left to right are (first row) Henry A. Braddy, Hugh B. Braddy, Moses Algerine Braddy, Florence Herndon Braddy, Betty Braddy Palmer, and Ruthie Braddy Phillips; (second row) Naomi Braddy Graham, Mamie Braddy Ricks, Annie Clyde Braddy Palmer, Dora Braddy Warnock, Alma Braddy Warnock, and Rufus Braddy; (third row) Oliver B. Braddy, William Braddy, and Eula Braddy.

A reunion of the Minnie Williamson Memory family was held about 1941 at Kibbee School. From left to right are (front row) Len Calhoun, Minedith Calhoun, Eton Hilton, J. H. Memory Jr., and Kay Memory; (second row) Agnes Calhoun, Jonnie Mae Hamilton, Jewel Williams, Tom Hilton, and Ruby Hilton; (third row) Arnold Calhoun, Kenneth Hamilton, Minnie Memory, Lucille Hamilton, and Helen Memory; (fourth row) Roy Calhoun, Sybil Williams, Rosa Hamilton, and Hilton Memory; (fifth row) Lovie Calhoun, Gene Hall, Editha Hall, James Williams, Renne Hall, Shelly Hamilton, Charles Hamilton, Lucille Hamilton, Alan Hall, and Rodney Allmond. (Courtesy of Kay Memory Claxton.)

Penelope Gillis Davis (1851-1911), a daughter of Neill Carmichael Gillis and Penelope Davis, married Thomas Andrew Davis Jr. (1849-1929) in 1871. Called "Singing Tom," he was a son of Thomas Andrew Davis and Cemantha McLendon. This couple reared at least 10 children. (Courtesy of Debra Fennell.)

Photographed in front of the Henry A. Braddy home are Reba Carmen Burns and Moses Algerine "M.A." Braddy. This picture was made in the 1940s.

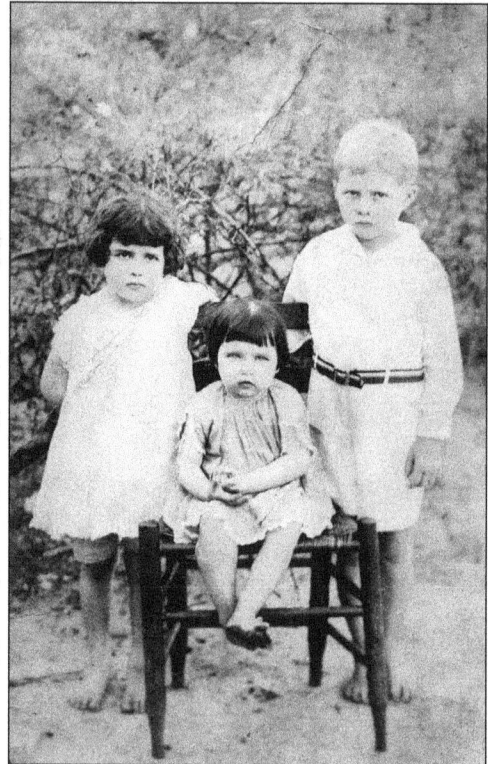

Posed here on a hot summer day in the yard of their home near Kibbee are, from left to right, Reba, Dot, and Jack Burns. They are children of Virgil Henry Burns and Mary Delilah Williamson. Note the running rose in the background. Virgil farmed in the Kibbee area on Tiger Creek for several years during the late 1930s.

Here Ruth Wilkes Phillips Wilkes (1885–1972) and her mother, Queen Ann Nunn Wilkes, appear to be taking a late afternoon stroll. Ruth Wilkes first married Meldrim Phillips, son of Dempsey C. Phillips and Delilah McLeod. He died at a young age, and she married Francis Malcolm Wilkes, son of John O. Wilkes and Catherine Shaw. Queen (1856–1946), daughter of Green Nunn and Sarah Lucinda Wilkes, was the widow of William Thomas Wilkes, son of Alexander Wilkes and Eliza Mosley. (Courtesy of Mary Achenbach Wilkes.)

Sarah Peterson was born in 1828 to Daniel Peterson and Mary O'Neal, who were among the first settlers of Montgomery County. In 1861, Sarah had a daughter, Laura Ann Peterson, who married James Jackson Fountain in 1885. Sarah made her home with the Fountains until her death in 1901. (Courtesy of Robert Calhoun.)

Malcolm Lee "Make" Adams (1876–1955) poses here with his second wife, the former Mary Jane Williamson, daughter of Andrew Jackson "Jack" Williamson and Lecy Ann Phillips. Make had first married Margaret "Maggie" Wheeler, and Mary's first husband was George W. Blocker. (Courtesy of Bobby T. Moore.)

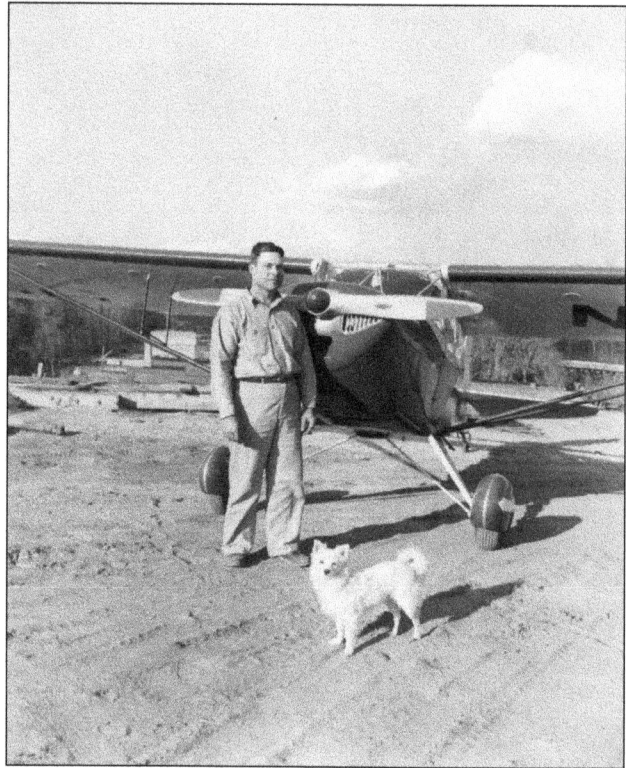

Thomas Lee Roy (or Leroy) Phillips (1908–1983) was quite a colorful character, and it appears he enjoyed life to its fullest. He is remembered best for daredevil stunts when flying his airplane. Roy and his wife, Nita Adams (1907–1997), made their home on the banks of the Altamaha River, where he fashioned a landing field for the airplane. When Georgia Power's Plant Hatch acquired the land, the couple was forced to abandon their home and move. Roy was a son of Thomas Jefferson Phillips and Quincey Lee Blaxton, and Nita was a daughter of Anthony Lindsey Adams and Ruth Elizabeth Williamson, members of some of the founding families of Montgomery County. (Courtesy of Bobby Tyson.)

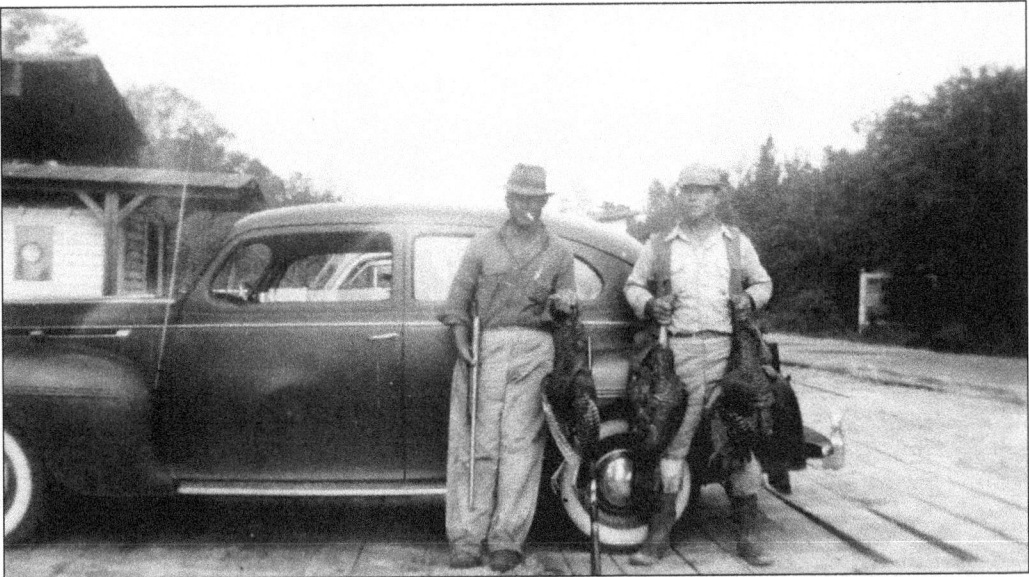

At a time when turkeys were thought to be almost extinct in the area, Roy Phillips and a companion appear to have had luck hunting them. The huge wooden bridge shown behind them is believed to be the old bridge across the Altamaha River. This picture was made in the 1930s. (Courtesy of Bobby Tyson.)

This is a rare funeral memorial for Ruth Hamilton, who died in 1907. Ruth Ann Elizabeth Williams was born in Tattnall County in 1844 and became the second wife of Charles Stringer Hamilton in 1865. To them were born 11 children, whose descendants are many in Montgomery and surrounding counties. (Courtesy of Bobby Tyson.)

Mary Jane Williamson shows off her stylish outfit in this picture made when she was in her teens. Born in 1885, she was one of 11 children born to Andrew Jackson Williamson II and Lecy Ann Phillips. In 1903, she married George W. Blocker (1881–1931), and after his death, she became the second wife of Malcolm Lee "Make" Adams (1876–1955). Mary is buried with her family in the Jack Williamson Cemetery near Kibbee. (Courtesy of Bobby Tyson and Gary Blocker.)

Posing in this baby picture is Hermon Williamson (1918–1998), son of John Hilton Williamson and Sadie Phillips. Hermon married Lillian Juanita Pollett (1920–1966), daughter of Frank Pollett and Ida Mae Twiggs. (Courtesy of Bobby Tyson.)

Ephron Jackson "E. J." Williamson (1904–1977) is captured in a cute studio pose. The oldest son of John Hilton Williamson and Sadie Phillips, he first married Jessie Jackson and then Eula Hammock. (Courtesy of Bobby Tyson.)

Mary Jane Williamson Blocker (1885–1964) is photographed here with her son, Thomas Alexander "T. A." Blocker (1911–1994). (Courtesy of Bobby Tyson.)

Probably made the day of their marriage in 1916, this photograph shows Lena Mabel O'Connor (1899–1956) posing beside her husband, James Leon "Jim" Memory (1897–1961). Mabel was a daughter of James Benjamin "J. B." O'Connor Jr. and Eliza Grace Palmer. This family lived in the Kibbee community. (Courtesy of Joseph Hilton Memory Jr.)

Almeda Williamson (1880–1966) is posed here in her teens in a lovely dress of the period. Note the pictures placed on the table in front of her. A daughter of Andrew Jackson "Jack" Williamson and Lecy Ann Phillips, she married Mack Franklin Davis (1877–1941). (Courtesy of Bobby Tyson.)

Pictured behind what appears to be a bear rug is James Leon "Jim" Memory (1897–1961) when a small boy. He was a son of John Anson Memory and Minnie Williamson. Note the dress worn by young boys of the period. (Courtesy of Joseph Hilton Memory Jr.)

Saphronia Collins (1893–1992) was the daughter of Mary Ann Elizabeth Adams and Sikes Collins. She married Columbus "Lummie" Collins, son of James Cannie Collins and Queen Ann America McCullough, of Cobbtown in Tattnall County. The couple lived in the Kibbee community all of their lives and farmed the property that Saphronia inherited from her parents. They were the parents of Melborne and Jewell Collins. Melborne never married. Jewell married Jason Cadwell "Cad" Edge, and they were the parents of Greg Edge of Tarrytown, who still lives in the house of his grandparents, and Gail Edge Claxton, who now lives in Augusta.

Shown around 1910 are Thelma Lugenia Hall (left) and her sister, Lavert Hall, daughters of Lyman "Boss" Hall and Teresa Williamson. Lugenia (1901–1977) married Benjamin Randolph "B. R." Page. Lavert (1905–1994) married Leroy Dickerson from lower Toombs County. (Courtesy of Mary Achenbach Wilkes.)

George Silas Blaxton (1864–1933) and his wife, Sara Ella Nunn (1866–1922), are pictured here later in life. George was a son of Argyle Blackstone and Hester Herrington, and Sarah was a daughter of Green Nunn and Sarah Lucinda Wilkes of the Taylor Springs community. George and Sarah were the parents of 12 children. (Courtesy of Bobby Tyson.)

George Washington Galbreath was the son of Daniel Webster Galbreath and Florence Clifton of the Sharpe Spur community in southeastern Montgomery County, where he was a prosperous farmer and the patriarch of a large family. In 1907, he married Ailey McGill, a daughter of Neil and Lurania McGill of the same vicinity. The couple reared 11 children on their farm. Many of their direct descendants continue to live on the ancestral property of their forebears. (Courtesy of Betty Burns Galbreath.)

Gladys Palmer Blaxton (1903–1924) was a daughter of Benjamin Franklin "Bennie" Palmer and Lavenia Williamson. She married William Mack Blaxton (1903–1987), son of George Silas Blaxton and Sara Ella Nunn. Gladys died of tuberculosis at the age of 21, leaving three small children, Thermon, Wilbert, and Alva Mae. Alva Mae, who was an infant when her mother died, was adopted by her mother's sister, Ebesta Palmer Shuman.

Perched on the bumper of his Model A, Thomas Jefferson Phillips (1887–1938) seems to waiting for someone to come take a ride with him. Thomas was one of 11 children of Ephraim B. and Ellen Phillips. He married Quincey Lee Blaxton in 1904. Their marriage ended in divorce. (Courtesy of Bobby Tyson.)

Isaac Larrimore Ladson (1854–1942) was born in Montgomery County to John Connoway Ladson and Mary Ann Calhoun, both natives of Barnwell County, South Carolina. In 1874, Isaac married Pinkey Grace Elizabeth Connell (1858–1917), daughter of William Connell and Pinkey Mosley. This couple reared 11 children in the Bear Creek community. They became the grandparents of the renowned John Elzie "Jack" Ladson Jr. (1912–1999), founder of the Ladson Genealogical Library in Vidalia, Georgia. (Courtesy of Bobby T. Moore.)

Outstanding women of Tarrytown pictured in this composite are (clockwise from top left) Beulah Barnes, Minnie Flanders, Mattie Lou Robinson, and Elnora Davis. These women are remembered as hard-working, God-fearing, and always ready to lend a helping hand, whether in their church or in their community. (Courtesy of Gary Blocker.)

Elizabeth Underwood (born c. 1847) and her daughter, Fannie Underwood Brantley, are taking time out of the day's work to stand for a picture beside their log house. Fannie Underwood (born 1881) became the wife of James A. J. Brantley (born 1872), and their daughter, Rebecca "Becky," married Willie V. McGahee and reared their family in the Kibbee community. (Courtesy of Annie Lou McGahee Edge.)

Roosevelt "Doodle" Mosley was a son of Tee and Gladys Mosley of the Mosley Town community near Tarrytown. He was known for his outstanding landscaping and horticultural abilities. (Courtesy of Gary Blocker.)

In this 1940s photograph, George Washington Hamilton (1877–1967), left, and Malcolm Lee "Make" Adams (1876–1955) appear to be admiring the quality of the cotton bale between them. (Courtesy of Gary Blocker.)

I. J. Brown (1919–1979) is proudly posing for a photograph with his bride, Gladys Whitley (1923–2009), daughter of Charlie Whitley and Lottie Mae Nix of Troup County, Georgia. I. J. was a son of James Lovett Brown and Alice Purvis. The couple is shown on the farm near Kibbee where they lived, farmed, and raised their children during the 1950s and 1960s. (Courtesy of Gary Blocker.)

The family of Henry Grady Walker (1897–1953) and Earnie Mae Hamilton (1898–1982) is shown in this 1930s pose. H. C. and Annie Estelle Walker were parents of Henry, and Earnie Mae's parents were Benjamin Franklin "Bennie" Hamilton and Effonia "Effie" Williamson. This family lived on the Old Louisville Road near Tarrytown. (Courtesy of Grady Mae Walker Simons.)

This picture of John Douglas "Doug" Williamson was probably taken about 1932, not long before his death at the age of 30—he was murdered by a kinsman over a keg of whiskey. Even though he had lost an arm in childhood in a cotton gin accident, he was said to be stronger and more muscular than most men. A son of Millard Milton Williamson and Mary Ann Delilah Adams, he was buried in the old Andrew J. Williamson Cemetery on present-day Georgia Highway 297. (Courtesy of Betty Burns Galbreath.)

Willie C. Cauley is pictured here with his sons, Preston (left) and Willie Cad "Sonny Man." They are proudly showing off a new litter of Walker foxhound puppies. The men of this family were known to be avid fox hunters. (Courtesy of Gary Blocker.)

In the 1970s, Onie Calhoun Williamson, right, presented to Brewton-Parker College a portrait of her father, Benjamin Stewart "Benny" Calhoun (1861–1951), who had been instrumental in the founding of its predecessor, Union Baptist Institute, in 1904 (it was renamed Brewton-Parker College in 1912). For the next 20 years, he served on the college's board of trustees, as well as various committees, including finance, prudential, auditing, and improvement.

Shown here in 1987, Onie Williamson's son, G. B. Williamson, and her granddaughter, Olivia Williamson Morris (now Braddy), are viewing the portrait, which hangs in the Fountain-New Library. They had been attending the Scottish games and dedication to the Calhoun family of Montgomery County, which was held on campus that day.

71

Elmira Estella "Stella" Collins Braddy (1885–1972) is portrayed here as a young woman. The daughter of Mary Ann Elizabeth Adams of Kibbee and Sikes Collins of Cobbtown, Tattnall County, Stella married Henry Algerine Braddy (1879–1955) in 1903. The couple lived for around 15 years on the maternal property of Henry in Montgomery County (Herndon land). In 1918, they moved their family to the homestead of her parents in northern Montgomery County. The grandchildren of Henry and Stella Collins Braddy still own this ancestral property. Stella was a noted genealogist and historian in her own right, possessing extensive knowledge of the families throughout Montgomery County.

Two

THEY SERVED
ADMIRABLY

William Riley Adams (1829–1918) fought in the War Between the States in Company G of the 32nd Georgia Regiment, for which he drew a pension later in life. He was described as 6 feet tall, of light complexion, with brown hair and blue eyes. The firstborn child of Asa Lemuel Adams and Louisa Phillips, William married Mary "Polly" Hamilton (1830–1900) in January 1849; she was a daughter of Josiah Hamilton and Mary "Polly" Poole. To this couple were born 19 children, but only 12 reached adulthood. William joined Bear Creek Church in August 1849; his father joined the next day, and they were baptized at the same time. In 1890, he sawed the lumber and helped to build Mt. Pisgah Baptist Church in Kibbee, where he had also built a large home for his family. (Courtesy of Jean Griffin Moore.)

73

Solomon Williamson was born in Montgomery County in 1823 to John and Elizabeth Sullivan Williamson. An entry in the court record book, *Inferior and Ordinary Court Minutes 1809–1849*, dated August 5, 1844, states "Solomon Williamson took oath of office for Deputy Sheriff of Montgomery County." He would have been almost 21 years of age and had already fought in the Florida Indian wars. Solomon went on to acquire thousands of acres of land in Emanuel County, where he settled near Oak Park and built a two-story log home. He served as an inferior court justice (holding court in his home) and served in Emanuel Troops for Local Defense during the War Between the States. Solomon first married Delila Trapnell in 1850, and after her death, he married Clarissa Calhoun of Tarrytown in 1876; he was the father of 18 children.

Willard McGill is pictured here in his World War I uniform. Willard was a son of Neil and Lurania McGill of Long Pond and Alston. (Courtesy of Betty Burns Galbreath.)

Posing for a photograph in his uniform during World War I is Benny Connell, son of John Neal Connell and Martha Blount of the Bear Creek community. (Courtesy of George King II.)

William Mosley (1839–1913), son of Seaborn Mosley and Margaret Moore, was a Confederate soldier from Montgomery County. He married Emma Eliza Braddy (1841–1923), daughter of Oliver Bennett Braddy and Elizabeth Smith. This family moved to Clay County, Florida.

William Thomas Ezekiel "W. T. E." Adams (1829–1907), son of Matthias Adams and Eliza Collins, fought in the War Between the States. He first married Delilah Frances Browning (1833–1899) and later married Delila Frances Wright Ryals.

Pictured here is George King during World War I. He was a son of John Ellis King and Christian Alice Connell. (Courtesy of George King II.)

Abbie Leon Wilkes is pictured here in his World War II uniform. A son of Eulie Green Wilkes and Martha Ella Taylor, he married Dorothy DeAlva Palmer Blaxton. (Courtesy of Mary Achenbach Wilkes.)

Shown here is a reunion held around 1918 in Vidalia, Georgia, of a group of local Confederate veterans. Among them is Jarred E. Palmer, who fought in Company C, 57th Georgia Regiment. Note the Southern Cross of Honor on each of their lapels. The Vidalia railroad station is in the background. (Courtesy of Mary Achenbach Wilkes.)

Charles Benton Parker was a successful businessman from McRae. According to Ann C. Turner, author of *Brewton-Parker College: Triumph Over Adversity, the First One-Hundred Years*, "Charles Benton Parker was born in Nansemond County (Virginia) on September 6, 1836. He was married to Sarah (Sallie) Matilda Howell, daughter of Rev. Edward Howell, on November 7, 1865. The Parkers relocated to Georgia in the 1870s." In 1904, John Carter Brewton, a Baptist pastor, cofounded the Union Baptist Institute in Montgomery County to provide elementary and secondary Christian education to children in South Georgia, and Parker provided financial assistance. The school was situated in Montgomery County, between the towns of Mount Vernon and Ailey. The school later became Brewton-Parker College, a four-year liberal arts college. (Courtesy of Ann C. Turner.)

Gerald Hope Achenbach (1910–1996) is pictured here receiving a medal of highest honor from the regent of the Vidalia chapter of the Daughters of the American Revolution, Gladys Rose Purvis Shuman. A native of Montana, Achenbach was a noted benefactor for many worthwhile projects in Montgomery and Toombs Counties. His name is more often associated with the chain of Piggly-Wiggly stores that originated in Vidalia and flourished throughout the South for decades. In 1949, he married Sarah Dean Jones (1912–1988) of Albany, Georgia, and they were the parents of Charles Henry, Gerald Hope Jr., Jane Towers, Mary Dean, Ann Towers, and John Wood. Achenbach often referred to himself as a "transplanted Southerner." (Courtesy of Mary Achenbach Wilkes.)

David A. Fountain (1866–1947) and his wife, Eliza A. O'Connor (1869–1953), gave much of their time and financial assistance to Brewton-Parker College, including 10 acres of land on which Union Baptist Institute (the forerunner of the college) was built in 1904. David was a son of James Isaac Fountain and Sabrina Chambers; Eliza was a daughter of James Benjamin "Jim" O'Connor and Clarissa Ann Hamilton. Their portraits now hang in the Fountain-New Library on the Brewton-Parker campus. (Courtesy of Ann C. Turner.)

Dr. Jarrett William Palmer (1874–1969) was practicing medicine in Mount Vernon as early as 1904. A son of William Tootle Palmer and Emma Dent, Dr. Palmer first married Laura Stella Riddle (1883–1935)and later married Eula Marie Peterson (1896–1984).

Dr. Hiram Chesley Sharpe (1883–1966) practiced medicine in the Alston and Uvalda communities in the early 1900s. He first married Ella Mae Ables, of Tennessee, with whom he is pictured here, probably on their wedding day. After her death, he married Ida Maryann Wilkes. (Courtesy of Wayne Wilkes.)

Posing here are cousins Herbert (left) and Bobby Burns. Herbert fought overseas during World War II, as well as in the Korean War; he was the son of Robert Lee Burns and Nettie Phillips. Bobby was the son of Virgil Henry Burns and Mary Delilah "Lila" Williamson; he served in the Korean War. (Courtesy of Herbert Burns.)

Hiram Galbreath (1919–1980), son of George Washington Galbreath and Ailey McGill, served in Europe in World War II. He married Betty Jane Burns, daughter of Virgil Henry Burns and Mary Delilah "Lila" Williamson. (Courtesy of Betty Burns Galbreath.)

Isaac Hart Beckworth (1842–1923) served the Confederacy during the War Between the States. A son of Ananias Beckworth and Elizabeth Tompkins, he was first married to Julia Ann Ansley Littleton, and after her death, he married Effie Anderson. He was 64 years of age when this picture was made. This family migrated to Henderson County, Texas.

Confederate veteran Jarred Edward "Ed" Palmer (1844–1928) is pictured here in midlife. Born in Laurens County to Jarred J. Irwin Palmer and Hephsebeth Livingston, he first married Martha Ann Hamilton (1842–1921) and by her had 12 children. In 1921, he married Clara Mae Fountain. (Courtesy of Mary Achenbach Wilkes.)

Lester Miles Blaxton (1895–1943) is posing here in his World War I uniform. A son of George Silas Blaxton and Sara Ella Nunn, he married Dorothy DeAlva Palmer (1910–1994) in 1929. They were the parents of DeAvis, Lester Miles Jr. "Buddy," and Myrna DeAnne. (Courtesy of Mary Achenbach Wilkes.)

Mattie Lou Robinson was a midwife who delivered over 1,000 babies in the Tarrytown community. She was a faithful member of Mount Nebo Church in Tarrytown. (Courtesy of the Robinson family.)

Nathaniel Alphus "Nathan" Adams (1832–1926), left, and William Riley Adams (1829–1918) were brothers who fought in the Confederate Army in the War Between the States. They were sons of Asa Lemuel Adams and Louisa Phillips. Nathan married Julia Ann Davis (1844–1926); William married Mary "Polly" Hamilton (1830–1900). (Courtesy of the Adams family.)

James Malichi McDonald (1847–1941), a Confederate veteran of the War Between the States, in which he served as sergeant in the 4th Georgia Cavalry, enlisting at the age of 13, is shown with his second wife, Ida Lucinda Calhoun Mosley (1883–1970). James first married Mary Melissa Jane Matthews (1851–1919). (Courtesy of John McDonald.)

Pictured in his World War I uniform is Riley Lutrell Adams (1898–1974), son of Charles Malcolm "Charlie" Adams and Mollie Hutcheson. Lutrell married Martha Moxley (1918–1985). When World War II was declared, he reenlisted and served again during this period. (Courtesy of Bobby Tyson and Bobby T. Moore.)

This full-length photograph shows another version of George King's World War I uniform. A son of John Ellis King and Christian Alice Connell, George fought in the overseas arena. (Courtesy of George King II.)

Three

HOMES OF YESTERYEAR

The William Riley Adams family is pictured in front of their home in Kibbee at a family reunion at the beginning of the 20th century. Descendants of this family have played a prominent role in the history of Montgomery County. (Courtesy of Bobby Tyson.)

Pictured here is the old McAllister house located on Old River Road. This house was built around 1850, probably by Samuel McAllister (1798–1863) or one of his sons. This family is buried across the road in the McAllister cemetery. (Courtesy of the Montgomery County Office of Clerk of Courts.)

J. J. "Tupper" and Honorine Moses are pictured here in front of their house on Old River Road near Uvalda. James Joshua Moses (1860–1935) was a son of Martin Thomas Moses and Mary Cook Conner; Honorine Louise Calhoun (1865–1959) was a daughter of William "Billy" Calhoun and Missouri McArthur. Honorine's line of Calhouns descends from her great-grandfather Angus Colquhoun, born 1782 in the Scottish Highlands, and is not related to the other Calhouns of Montgomery County. This photograph was made in the early 1900s. (Courtesy of the Montgomery County Office of Clerk of Courts.)

The Chesley McLemore house was built around 1864. Located on Old Savannah Road near Vidalia, it is estimated that the exposed beams were made from trees about 125 years old, at the time it was built. This cabin is listed on the National Register of Historic Places. Chesley Bostwick McLemore (1813–1899), son of John Howell McLemore, married Elizabeth "Lizzie" Thigpen (1823–1909), daughter of Melancthon Thigpen and Barbara Ann Ricks. (Courtesy of the Montgomery County Office of Clerk of Courts.)

Inez Sharpe McGregor is shown here inspecting her grandmother's loom in the Chesley McLemore house. She was a daughter of Robert Lee "Bob" Sharpe and Eliza Jane McLemore and grew up next-door to this historic old home. (Courtesy of the Montgomery County Office of Clerk of Courts.)

Shown here is the McCall house near Swift Creek. The boy in the wagon is Lawrence McCall. (Courtesy of Lawrence McCall.)

Near Kibbee stood the home of Lloyd Conaway (1915-1998) and his family. Lloyd was a son of Wiley Alex Conaway and Callie Belle Warnock. He first married Nellie Powell in 1936, and in 1977 married Iva Lee Edwards. Note the large woodpile, necessary for heating and cooking, and the rain barrel beside the house. This house has been torn down in recent months. (Courtesy of Faye Conaway Waller.)

This was the first house of Lee and Mary Esta Moore at the intersection of Old Kibbee Road and Thompson Pond Road. It was built in the early 1900s. (Courtesy of Doris Davis Moore.)

Robert Lee "Bob" Sharpe built this house in 1903 near the home of his father-in-law, Chesley McLemore. This farmhouse still has many of its outbuildings, including the smokehouse, chicken house, and washhouse, and is listed on the National Register of Historic Places. (Courtesy of the Montgomery County Office of Clerk of Courts.)

The McRae house in Mount Vernon is a typical Victorian house. It was built by Duncan A. McRae and still stands, being used now as a convalescent home. (Courtesy of Philip McRae.)

Considered to be the oldest house in Montgomery County and known as the Cooper-Conner house, this log cabin was built for Richard Cooper, a Revolutionary soldier, around 1779. The house is pictured here in its original location on Old River Road near Dead River. It has since been donated by Don McArthur and moved to the campus of Brewton-Parker College, where it is part of the historic village. (Courtesy of the Montgomery County Office of Clerk of Courts.)

This picture of a family reunion was taken in 1902 at the old homeplace of Martin and Nancy Hightower. Martin, born and reared in Washington County, served the Confederacy in the War Between the States. In 1858, he married Nancy Palmer, a daughter of Jarred J. Irwin Palmer and Hephsebeth Livingston of Laurens County. Martin is shown on the second row, center, in the black coat; Nancy is to his left in the striped dress. (Courtesy of Lawrence McCall.)

The old log house of Johnny McQueen still stands between Higgston and Vidalia. The front part of the house was built of logs, and after a time, the kitchen was built behind it, with a covered walkway connecting it to the main house. (Courtesy of Lawrence McCall.)

Shown is an aerial view of the Wiley B. Phillips/Larry R. Braddy house. Built in 1892 from yellow, virgin heart pine cut on the farm and dry-kilned on the hillside in front of the house, this structure is a typical Victorian home with a wraparound porch. The Phillips/Braddy house is considered a landmark of old Montgomery County.

Shown is the W. A. Conaway family in front of their home on Taylor Springs Road. Wiley Alex Conaway (1880–1965) was a son of Asa D. Conaway and his first wife, Cornelia. He married Callie Belle Warnock (1879–1962), daughter of Christopher Columbus "Lum" Warnock and Margam Adams. In later years, their son Cecil and his family lived here. This house has free-standing columns at the front porch. (Courtesy of Faye Conaway Waller.)

Four

LIFE ON THE FARM

Shown are members of the Sharpe family posing with an oxcart. The team of oxen was called Maude and Pearl. The picture was made on the Sharpe farm near Alston. (Courtesy of Wayne Wilkes.)

A noted equestrian of Montgomery County, Athel Braddy is posing here with one of his prize horses. Wallace Athel Braddy (1920–1968) was born in Montgomery County to Henry Algerine Braddy and Elmira Estella Collins. He married Letitia Lowman in 1939. (Courtesy of Billy Wade Jr.)

Benjamin Chess "B. C." and Emma Moxley are shown here in their cotton field in the Taylor Springs community. Cotton has been a staple crop in Montgomery County for generations. In the early days, horse or mule-drawn planters were used to plant and plow the crop. Farmers and their families chopped and thinned the plants. Later, cotton was harvested by hand and placed in cotton sacks of burlap. Cotton-picking machines now harvest cotton on a large scale throughout the county. (Courtesy of Rubie Nell Moxley Sanders.)

Shown in this 1930 picture are George Washington Galbreath and his grandchild, of the Sharpe Spur community. George was a prominent farmer in his community and relied on his mules for the production of crops. George was the son of Daniel Webster Galbreath and Florence Clifton. He married Ailey McGill of Sharpe Spur. Their descendants still own the family farm. (Courtesy of Betty Burns Galbreath.)

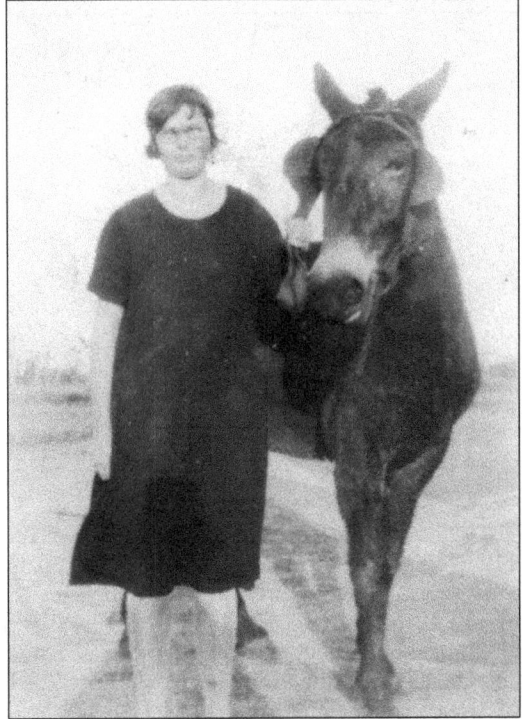

Shown in this 1930s photograph with her mule, Katie, is Beatrice Cooper McGahee, who lived near Kibbee in northern Montgomery County. Beatrice and her husband, Lee McGahee, farmed in the area for many years. Mules served as an essential beast of burden on the farms in Montgomery prior to the introduction of the tractor and modern farm implements. (Courtesy of Annie Lou McGahee Edge.)

John R. Adams (left) and an unidentified friend are pictured with a log cart and team of oxen in front of the Adams barn in this c. 1895 tintype. John Robert Adams was a son of W. T. E. Adams and Mary Delilah Browning. Not only were horses and mules used for the production of crops, but they were used extensively, along with oxen, in the harvesting of huge virgin pine trees that covered the wiregrass woodlands of the county. John R. Adams, who lived to be 102 years of age, worked on the farm and in the woods, where he cut down huge pine trees and dragged them to the Oconee River and rafted them down the Altamaha to Darien for shipment to markets abroad. (Courtesy of Theresa Adams Tomlinson.)

This is the old homeplace of Angus McQueen and his wife, Harriet McMillan, located just north of Higgston. The picture was taken between 1889 (Angus's death) and 1902 (Harriet's death). From left to right are (standing in the yard) Ernie Smith, Effie McQueen Smith, Lilly Smith Hamilton, Lizzie McQueen Allmond, and Sara Smith; (sitting on the porch) Robert McMillan and Harriet McMillan McQueen. Mr. Britt, the hired man, is standing with the horse and buggy. (Courtesy of Lawrence McCall.)

Prior to modern indoor plumbing, the outdoor privy was an essential feature on every homestead in Montgomery County. This outdoor privy was on the Lloyd Conaway farm near Kibbee in northern Montgomery County. (Courtesy of Faye Conaway Waller.)

This photograph, made in the 1930s, of a farm woman pumping water captures a typical example of the many daily chores expected of each member of the family. This type of pump was the forerunner of the electric pump, and although it would seem like hard work to women of today, it was actually much easier than drawing water up from the well with a rope and bucket. The woman, whose name is unknown, was a member of either the Adams or Ryals family. (Courtesy of Theresa Adams Tomlinson.)

The production of wheat in Montgomery provided flour for the table. Several gristmills in the area processed wheat into flour. This old photograph shows the processing of wheat. Now huge combines have eliminated many of the steps previously required in the harvesting of wheat. This wheat field was near Uvalda. (Courtesy of the Montgomery County Office of Clerk of Courts.)

The production of cotton in Montgomery has provided the county's farming cash over the centuries, despite the arduous task of growing it. Shown here is Pearl R. Hamilton (center), showing his "bale to the acre" crop to Claude C. McDonald (left) and James R. Adams near the village of Kibbee. (Courtesy of the Montgomery County Office of Clerk of Courts.)

The harvesting and marketing of virgin pine trees in the pine barrens of Montgomery County provided the settlers with income. Huge pines were felled, dragged to the Oconee and Altamaha Rivers, and floated to the port at Darien for shipment to markets in Europe and Asia. Shown are settlers preparing a large raft of pines for the long, tedious trip downstream to the sea. (Courtesy of the Montgomery County Office of Clerk of Courts.)

The production of tobacco in Montgomery after World War II provided a cash crop for the county's farmers. The federal government provided each farmer with an allotment of tobacco. In the early days of the production of tobacco, the tender transplants were painstakingly set by hand with manual transplanting implements. The leaves were harvested when the plants reached maturity. "Putting in tobacco," a labor-intensive task, required the assistance of family and neighbors. Later, the sticks of tobacco were cured in barns like the one shown here on the Conaway farm near Kibbee. (Courtesy of Faye Conaway Waller.)

Five

PUBLIC LANDMARKS

In 1863, an oak was planted at the grave of a slave girl by her master, Robert Troup, brother of former governor George M. Troup. The tombstone, which was located on one of the original Troup plantations south of Glenville, reads "Sacred to the memory of Milly Troup who departed this life on the 8th day of Oct. 1863. Aged 22 years." The huge oak still shades the girl's grave, in accordance with its planter's instructions. (Courtesy of the Montgomery County Office of Clerk of Courts.)

Pictured here is the Higgston depot. Higgston, located in eastern Montgomery County near Vidalia, was a railroad town and thriving community with several churches, a school, stores, and a large hotel. The old depot served as the hub of commercial activity, including a passenger train to Macon and Savannah. (Courtesy of Marian Witt Hutcheson.)

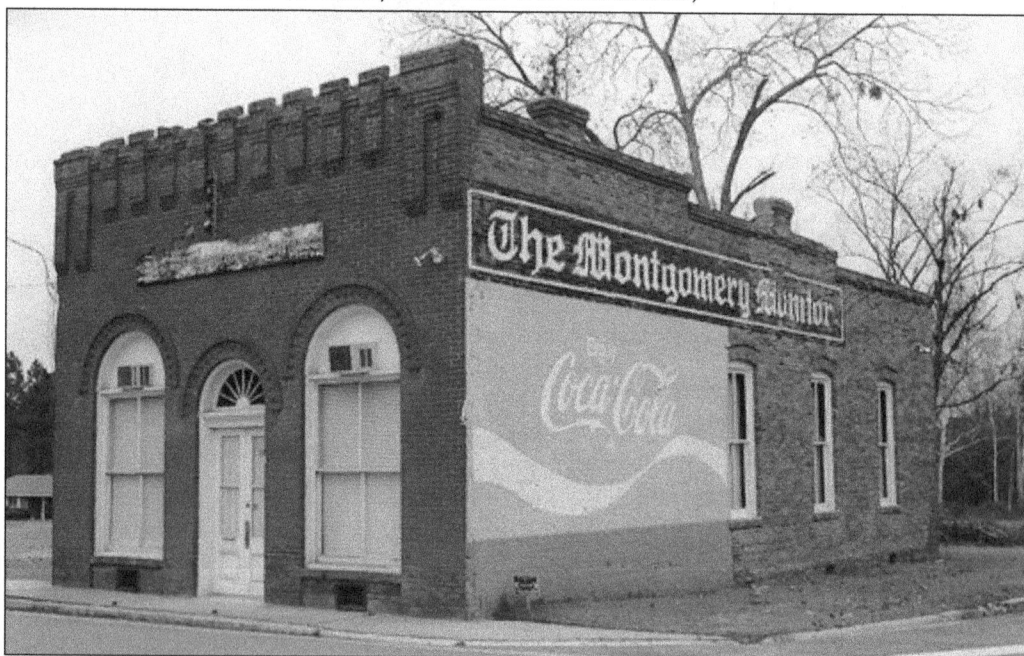

The building shown in this old photograph housed the *Montgomery Monitor* for many decades and still stands in downtown Mount Vernon. The *Montgomery Monitor* is the region's oldest newspaper and continues to serve as the source of much of the county's news and history.

William A. McQueen's general store in Mount Vernon is pictured here in 1897. School was dismissed to watch laying of the corner stone for the store, which was the first brick building in Mount Vernon. The upper floor was used as the Masonic lodge hall and later became Pal Movie Theater. (Courtesy of the Montgomery County Office of Clerk of Courts.)

The cotton gin in Kibbee is shown here at the beginning of the 20th century. Kibbee, a railroad town on the Macon, Dublin, and Savannah Railroad, was a bustling commercial community with several stores and a railroad depot. The old cotton gin was adjacent to the depot. (Courtesy of Bobby Tyson.)

Pictured is a public hanging near Mount Vernon on September 19, 1893. Lucien Manuel, Hiram Jacobs, Hiram Brewington, Weldon Gordon, and Purse Strickland (not necessarily in that order) are standing on the gallows just prior to being hanged. The man fourth from left, with his hand resting on the gallows, is probably Sheriff George W. Dunham. The doomed men, called Scuffletonians (a mixture of Native American, black, and white races), from North Carolina, were guilty of various murders committed in Montgomery County earlier that year. The photograph is by A. H. Prince, a traveling photographer. (Courtesy of the Montgomery County Office of Clerk of Courts.)

Shown in this old photograph is the store owned around 1930 by Kibbee entrepreneur Robert Bennett "Rob" Wheeler (1898–1990), who dealt in tires and general merchandise. The adopted son of Malcolm Lee "Make" Adams and his wife, Maggie Wheeler, he married Agnes Odom (1907–1992). Rob Wheeler became successful in many activities, including farming, business, and horticulture. The gentleman in the picture is an unidentified representative of Giant Tires. (Courtesy of Gary Blocker.)

This earlier Montgomery County courthouse, built in 1854, is pictured around 1910. Note the men all dressed in business suits, in stark contrast to today's casual dress style. (Courtesy of the Montgomery County Office of Clerk of Courts.)

The front room of the home of Robert David "Bob" Beaty and his family served as a post office for the community known as May. This picture was made in 1900. From left to right are (on the steps) Benjamin Samuel "Benny," Anna Lou, Leila, and Susan Frances; (on the porch) Bob, Mattie Mae, Viola, and Lillian Ellowease. Children later born into the Beaty family were Robbie Lee, Grady, Otis Easter, Robert Eschol, Wilma Eudene, Rounell, and Bobbie Rae; several of these died in childhood. Robert David Beaty (1868–1941) was a son of James Andrew Beaty and Myriah Johnson; Viola Lydia Calhoun Beaty (1868–1936) was a daughter of Samuel Hargroves Calhoun and Mary Lucinda Hamilton. This old structure still stands and is currently owned by the couple's great-granddaughter, Sonja Braddy Spivey. (Courtesy of Sonja Braddy Spivey.)

Thomas Alexander "T. A." Blocker (1911–1994), one of Montgomery County's most prominent merchants, stands in his store in Kibbee, where he began his business under the sponsorship of Malcolm Lee "Make" Adams during the 1930s. In 1932, T. A. married Jimmie Durden (1915–2001), daughter of Harrison W. Durden and Priscilla Frost. He later moved his store to Georgia Highway 29 near Kibbee where his son, Gary Blocker, continues to operate it to this day. (Courtesy of Gary Blocker.)

Lamar Waller (right), a longtime merchant of Tarrytown, in northern Montgomery County, is shown here with an unidentified representative of the Georgia Forestry Commission, who bought pine cones gathered by local boys and sold to Lamar for spending money. The pine cones were used for seedlings in the reforestation of the county and state. (Courtesy of Faye Conaway Waller.)

Six

PLACES OF LEARNING AND WORSHIP

This 1906 picture of the Union Baptist Institute shows how rural the area still was at the time the school was built. The Union Baptist Institute was a high school attended by many children from Montgomery County families, including the Calhoun, McAllister, McArthur, and Hamilton families. The school later became Brewton-Parker College. The buildings shown are Gates Hall and the academic building. (Courtesy of the Montgomery County Office of Clerk of Courts.)

Ailey School, located near the old sawmill, is pictured here in 1914. Those identified are, in no particular order, (first row) Alex Peterson, Maggie Peterson, and Marie Peterson; (third row) Hoke Riddle, Ala Peterson, and Jessie Peterson; (fourth row) Boots Riddle, Collie Thompson, and Jim Stacy; (back row) on left, Willie Peterson. (Courtesy of the Montgomery County Office of Clerk of Courts.)

Dr. Hiram Sharpe (center) is pictured in 1912 showing off his new car. The man standing on the running board is K. M. Johnson; the other gentleman in the car is unidentified. Behind them is Dog Scratch School, located near Uvalda in the early 1900s. (Courtesy of Wayne Wilkes.)

This appears to be a class picture made at the door of the "new" Kibbee School, probably in the 1940s.

This photograph, taken in April 1956, depicts students happily leaving at the end of the day at Kibbee High School. The school is no longer in operation, and children in this community now attend school in Mount Vernon. (Courtesy of Gary Blocker.)

This old tintype is probably of Poplar Head School, located on the Thompson Pond Road near the farms of Henry Algerine Braddy and Benjamin Warnock. The teachers, including a Mrs. Price, boarded with the families of Henry A. Braddy, Charlie Collins, and Ben Warnock. M. A. Braddy was among the students who attended this old school. Note the log edifice. (Courtesy of Faye Conaway Waller.)

Pictured here is the old Memory Schoolhouse, located across the road from the home of John and Minnie Williamson Memory. Many children in the neighborhood attended this two-room school during the 1880s and 1890s, including the children from the Collins, Warnock, Memory, and Council families. The old structure still stands. (Courtesy of Bobby Tyson.)

This is Long Pond School around 1897. Seated are teacher I. C. Jenkins and assistant teacher Anna McArthur Rackley. Ada McArthur Peterson Willbanks is standing behind the bicycle. (Courtesy of the Montgomery County Office of Clerk of Courts.)

Mount Vernon High School is shown in this old picture, taken long after it ceased to be used as a school. The old building was used from 1880 to 1905, at which time the students were moved to Union Baptist Institute. Children from the pioneer families attended this historic school, including the Hughes, Flanders, Fountain, McAllister, and Mason families. The building still stands on Washington Street in Mount Vernon (formerly Old River Road). (Courtesy of the Montgomery County Office of Clerk of Courts.)

Baptismal services for Tarrytown Baptist Church were held at the Bennie Hamilton Pond near Tarrytown for many years. This photograph is typical of a Southern country church's baptizing. (Courtesy of Faye Conaway Waller.)

This is Mabel Burns's class at the old Kibbee School in approximately 1923. M. A. Braddy is shown third from right in the first row. (Courtesy of Faye Conaway Waller.)

Students are posing at the corner of the school in Ailey in this 1912 photograph. (Courtesy of the Montgomery County Office of Clerk of Courts.)

Shown here are the Sunday school classes in front of the Tarrytown Baptist Church around 1941. Among those portrayed are the Warnock, Phillips, and Waller children. The teachers in this old picture are Millard Phillips, Ruthie Braddy Phillips, Alma Braddy Warnock, and Lamar Waller. (Courtesy of Grace Warnock Dover.)

Pictured in this *c.* 1925 photograph of Kibbee School children are (in order of the numbers previously written directly on the picture) Mary Ruth Beckum, Clement Montford, Nadine Rewis, Hortense Palmer, Lula Mae Newton, Alberta West, Estelle Hammock, Margaret Moore, Editha Hamilton, Estelle Calhoun, Randolph Calhoun, Lloyd Conaway, J. W. Warnock, Fannis Humphrey, Douglas McCaw, Deen Mosley, Florence Braddy, unidentified, Claude Blocker, Wiley Williamson, Aubrey Stephens, Tom Watson Adams, Ladson Moore, and Van Braddy. (Courtesy of Gary Blocker.)

In this *c.* 1920 photograph, an unidentified worker is taking a rest on the doorstep of the old school in Alston. (Courtesy of Wayne Wilkes.)

Dale McDaniel is portrayed in this school photograph at the Alston School, where she taught the sixth and seventh grades for several decades. Her students held her in the highest esteem for her excellence in teaching. (Courtesy of Betty Burns Galbreath.)

Mrs. Blocker's class at the old Kibbee School is pictured here in approximately 1925. Among those identified, but not in any particular order, are M. A. Braddy, Preston Hamilton, Gary Smith, Mary Ella Hightower, Veda Smith, Helen Hilton, Nealie Ruth Youmans, Bruce Cauley, Royce ?, Aldine Moxley, Sadie McDonald, Ida Moxley, Madie McDonald, William Collins, Eileen Calhoun, Lila ?, Lucindy Allmond, Bonnie Palmer, Jimmie Durden, Eunice West, Reba King, Hattie Braddy, Muriel Allmond, Doris ?, Lucy Rae McDonald, Cornelia Whitaker, Charlie Selph, J. B. Selph, Robert Lee Simons, William Hamilton, J. C. Palmer, Herbert Memory, and Curtis Gay. (Courtesy of Gary Blocker.)

The Academic Building at the Union Baptist Institute (later Brewton-Parker College) is shown in this 1908 photograph. It was one of the oldest buildings on the Brewton-Parker College campus and housed the administrative suite; the old auditorium was upstairs. (Courtesy of the Montgomery County Office of Clerk of Courts.)

Mount Pisgah Baptist Church, located in Kibbee, is shown in this old photograph prior to the major renovation of the building. The land and lumber used in the construction of the sanctuary for this landmark church were donated by members of the William Riley Adams and Josiah Hamilton families, who were among the charter members of this historic church. (Courtesy of Marian Witt Hutcheson.)

It is believed that the congregation of Long Pond Methodist Church held services as early as 1793; however, it was not formally organized until 1850, the original name then being Salem Church. The church was relocated and renamed in 1877. The building shown in this picture was completed in 1901. (Courtesy of the Montgomery County Office of Clerk of Courts.)

Glenwood Methodist Episcopal Church is pictured here. The Methodists began meeting in a log building a half-century before the town of Glenwood came to be. In 1875, land was given by A. Morrison, and the original Methodist church was built. It was used as a school as well as a place of worship. After the first church burned, this church was built by Warren Pope with hand-sawn timbers. (Courtesy of the Montgomery County Office of Clerk of Courts.)

Visit us at
arcadiapublishing.com

www.ingramcontent.com/pod-product-compliance
Lightning Source LLC
Chambersburg PA
CBHW050702110426

42813CB00007B/2056